Great Events

REMEMBRANCE DAY

Written and Illustrated
by Gillian Clements

W
FRANKLIN WATTS
LONDON•SYDNEY

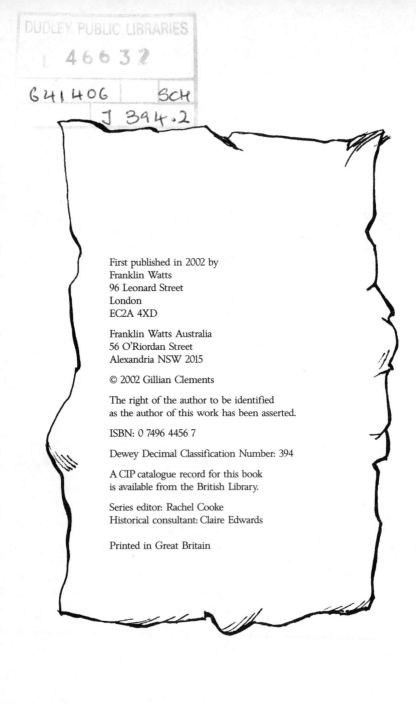

First published in 2002 by
Franklin Watts
96 Leonard Street
London
EC2A 4XD

Franklin Watts Australia
56 O'Riordan Street
Alexandria NSW 2015

ISBN: 0 7496 4456 7

Dewey Decimal Classification Number: 394

A CIP catalogue record for this book
is available from the British Library.

Series editor: Rachel Cooke
Historical consultant: Claire Edwards

Printed in Great Britain

REMEMBRANCE DAY

On cold, misty November mornings, every year, crowds of people come together to remember young men and women who fought and died in the Great War ... and later wars.

All kinds of people gather together on Remembrance Day. As the vicar speaks, they grow silent.

"At the eleventh hour, on the eleventh day of the eleventh month, we have come here to remember those who gave their lives in the Great War ... and all the wars that followed."

The Great War from 1914 to 1918 was called the "War to End All Wars". In those four terrible years, eight million soldiers met their deaths fighting for their countries.

Though the war began in Europe, it drew in armies from every corner of the world. No continent escaped its terrible destruction.

The Great War's story began in Sarajevo, Serbia, on 28th June 1914. A young Serb, Gavrilo Princip, rushed from a crowd, as a gleaming black car passed by. "BANG! BANG!" In a moment the car's passengers – Archduke Franz Ferdinand of Austria and his wife – lay dead.

Archduke Franz Ferdinand was heir to the throne of the vast Austria-Hungarian Empire. Of course, the Austrians were furious with the Serbs for killing him.

They declared war on Serbia. So Russia, Serbia's friend, declared war on the Austrians.

France supported the Russians. On 1st August, Germany joined in too, lining up with the Austrians and declaring war on Russia and France.

It was like a row of toppling dominoes. When the Germans invaded Belgium on their way to attack France, Britain entered the fight. Most of Europe was at war.

Everywhere, young men seemed eager to fight for their countries. They were ready for war and adventure!

"We don't want to lose you, but we think you ought to go!" sang Britain's Music Hall singers. And newspapers called on patriotic Englishmen, Scotsmen, Welshmen and Irishmen to enlist and fight the German "Hun".

"If we do not join the war, then Germany will rule the seas, and all Europe!" one politician declared.

"It will be a short war if we strike quickly," the generals promised.

But a few people called conscientious objectors refused to fight. "We cannot kill people," they said. Newspapers called them "hordes of cowards". Mostly people agreed with the war.

The armies lined up to fight each other. They fell into two camps: the Central Powers – Austria, Germany and Turkey – and the Allies – France, Britain, Russia, Italy and Japan. Each army made its way to the Fronts, the battle lines where they would fight.

Fighting soon began in Europe and in countries and colonies around the world – even in Africa, Samoa and New Guinea! India sent one and a half million volunteers to help its ruler, Britain. Africans fought too, for whichever European country controlled them – it could be for France, Britain or Germany.

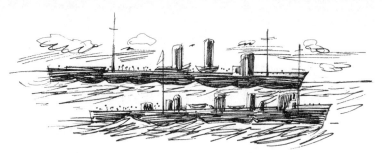

Now, thousands of British soldiers crossed the Channel to Belgium, and with their French allies, faced the German army on the Western Front. In the Belgian countryside at Mons, Marne and Ypres, each army dug long narrow ditches, called trenches, where they could shelter from enemy fire.

The Great War will always be remembered for its "trench warfare". Sometimes the trenches stretched over 1,000 kilometres.

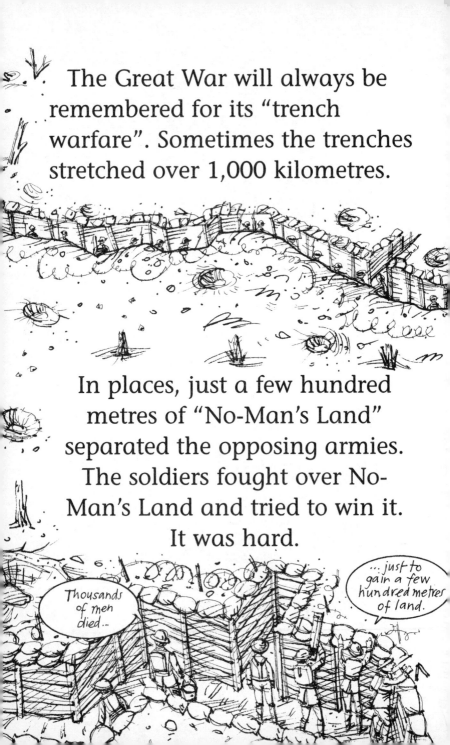

In places, just a few hundred metres of "No-Man's Land" separated the opposing armies. The soldiers fought over No-Man's Land and tried to win it. It was hard.

Thousands of men died...

...just to gain a few hundred metres of land.

Trenches were not the only creation of the Great War. There were many new weapons, too. From the start, the Germans had rifles, grenades and new German machine guns. British

"Those machine guns are overrated," said Britain's General Haig. But soon his soldiers had machine guns, too.

Machine guns? Stuff and nonsense!

To help them win, each side tried ever more deadly weapons – planes, tanks and gas. In 1915, the Germans attacked with gas. One gas made the soldiers choke and gasp, another burnt their skin or blinded them. "This is not war, it is the ending of the world," said one Indian soldier.

In the skies above, aeroplanes dropped bombs, or fired on enemy lines with machine guns. Back in Britain, the First Lord of the Admiralty, Winston Churchill, had an idea: "We need steam tractors! These armoured tanks could cross trenches, and break through the Hun's barbed wire." And so another deadly weapon entered the war.

At sea, Allied battleships blockaded Germany's coast. "If no food or fuel gets through," they reasoned, "then the German people will have to surrender."

But the German navy fought back! In 1915, Admiral Scheer's terrifying underwater U-boats torpedoed and sank hundreds of British and neutral ships.

Our U-boat submarines will bring a victorious end to the war.

On land, trench warfare was horrible, especially in winter. Cold, wet soldiers crouched in their filthy dugouts. Sometimes they shared their trenches with rats and dead comrades. In no time, fit young men fell ill with trench foot, trench fever and dysentery.

Out in No-Man's Land, heavy guns had blasted trees to stumps and carved out muddy craters.

"ATTACK!" Shouted orders sent soldiers scrambling over the top of the trenches. They struggled to advance across No-Man's Land. Their heavy loads dragged them deep into the sticky mud, while close to enemy lines, they became snagged on coils of barbed wire.

There's nowhere to hide.

A single machine gun could kill hundreds of soldiers in minutes.

Casualties – the number of soldiers wounded or killed – grew by the day. By Christmas 1914, there were more than 650,000 German casualties, about a million French, and nearly 100,000 British. But still no army could break through enemy lines.

But on the Great War's first Christmas Eve, the guns were silent for a time. Softly at first, a beautiful tune drifted in the darkness, towards the British lines. German soldiers were singing.

On Christmas Day, a few brave soldiers left their trenches to greet the enemy in No-Man's Land. Some played football. Then they exchanged cap badges or plum pudding. One German shook an Indian soldier's hand. "My God, why can't we have peace," he said, "and let us all go home!"

But in a day or two the killing started again.

It seemed no army had a big enough weapon to win the war. Casualties kept growing and death became normal. When the Germans attacked Verdun in France in 1916, each side lost half a million men.

"England will have to accustom herself to far greater losses before we finally crush the German army," said one officer.

What does it matter? There are plenty more men in England!

Again and again, in different battles and places, men fought bravely for little or no gain.

In 1915 at Gallipoli in Turkey, British and French troops, young Australians and New Zealanders, struggled up a steep hill to attack the Turks. They fought for six months before the Allies retreated, having lost 47,750 men. The Turks had won the battle, but they lost even more men: 55,000.

The war, the noise of shells and the terrible sights of death drove men to despair. Some harmed themselves to get out of the war. But Allied generals still ordered their men on to the attack.

Sometimes a few soldiers protested and refused to fight. But soldiers could be shot if they disobeyed orders.

At the Battle of the Somme in France in 1916, there were 650,000 Allied casualties (Britons, Frenchmen, Australians, New Zealanders and South Africans) ... and 500,000 German casualties.

Next year at Passchendaele, Canadians and other Allies lost 320,000 men – dead and wounded – for just 8 kilometres of land.

As the war dragged on, it was friends, letters from home, rum and free cigarettes, that kept most soldiers happy and sane. They sang and made up funny new words for hymns, to raise a laugh.

In Britain, on the Home Front, the war had been popular at first. But then people heard about the trenches and casualties. By 1917, seven million soldiers from many countries had died. The wounded total was forty-five million. Politicians told the women: "Keep the home fires burning… till the boys come home!" But millions of men would never return.

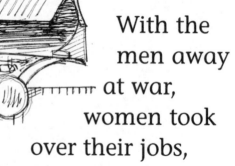

With the men away at war, women took over their jobs, doing a "man's work" in factories and offices. Many women worked as nurses and ambulance drivers as well.

As the war continued, there were food shortages and rationing. It was a difficult time for everyone.

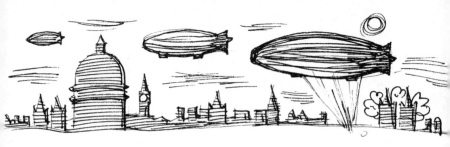

Though far from the battlefield, civilians were not always safe. Some passenger ships were sunk, and in the autumn of 1916, airships appeared over England. These Zeppelins from Germany dropped hundreds of bombs over Kent and London. People fled their homes for safety.

In Germany in 1917, many people starved and some died. Their home potato crop had failed the year before, and there was nothing to eat but turnips.

They still hoped for victory. And so did their enemy. But now everyone longed for peace.

In the war, some things were changing. The Russians made peace with the Germans. But now America, angry that Germany had torpedoed and sunk of some of its ships, joined the war. Its fit young soldiers were arriving to help the Allied cause.

The Germans fought on, but it was clear they could not win. In 1918, on 9th November, they began to discuss a peace agreement, called an armistice, and the German government finally admitted defeat. They signed the armistice on the morning of 11th November in a railway carriage near Compiègne, France.

Peace at last! At 11a.m., the fighting stopped. The victors rejoiced, shouting and dancing in the streets. Church bells pealed, and happy Canadian soldiers lit a bonfire in London's Trafalgar Square. In France, Parisians celebrated the victory all day and all night.

In 1919, in Paris, countries formed a League of Nations to try to stop future wars. Then politicians signed the Treaty of Versailles, to end the war properly.

With peace, soldiers returned to their families – and to work, if they could. But many carried the scars of war – blinded, gassed or still terrified of noise. People said they were shell-shocked.

"After this," people agreed, "there must never be another war." They tried to live a normal life and forget the horrors. But the English poet, Siegfried Sassoon, wrote sadly:

"Have you forgotten yet?
Look down, and swear by the slain
of the War that you'll never forget."

So, countries made monuments and memorials. Some remembered the "victory of right and freedom" over Germany. But most remembered the terrible losses. On their memorials they wrote, "Lest We Forget."

LEST WE FORGET

Britain's King George V spoke in 1919: "Let the people observe two minutes' silence at eleven o'clock on the morning of 11th November … in memory of the victims of war, and the declaration of peace!" And so they did. On that first anniversary of the end of the fighting, people bowed their heads in silence. Even the trains and cars stopped.

Every year since, countries have put aside a day for "remembrance". Many people in the British Commonwealth wear blood-red poppies on their Remembrance Day. After a terrible battle early in the war, John McCrae, a Canadian doctor, wrote:

"In Flanders fields the poppies blow
Between the crosses, row on row..."

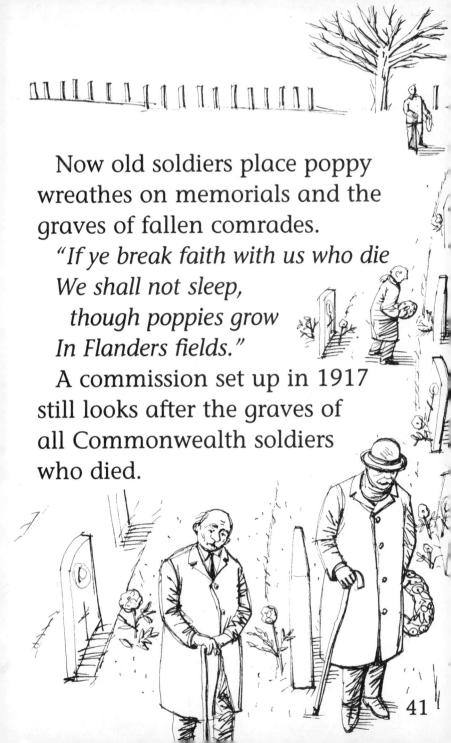

Now old soldiers place poppy wreathes on memorials and the graves of fallen comrades.

"If ye break faith with us who die
We shall not sleep,
though poppies grow
In Flanders fields."

A commission set up in 1917 still looks after the graves of all Commonwealth soldiers who died.

41

The first Remembrance Day remembered the end of the Great War. But many wars have been fought since then. The Great War was renamed the First World War in 1939, when the Second World War began. Sadly, there is nearly always a war somewhere in the world – and many war cemeteries filled with the fallen of many nations.

Most of these peaceful places are on land – in Flanders' Fields, or in Gallipoli, or on the Sussex Downs, where a "Chattri" reminds us of Indian Sikhs and Hindus killed in the First World War. Some are at sea, like the wreck of HMS Hood, whose crew of 1,300 drowned in the Second World War.

Whenever "Remembrance Days", "Armistice Days", "Veterans' Days" or "Memorial Days" are observed around the world – they remember the loss of life. They honour the dead of all the wars, but they also celebrate and pray for peace.

World Remembrance Days

 **Australia:** ANZAC Day, 25th April; Remembrance Day, 11th November

Canada: Remembrance Day, 11th November

 France: *Jour de Souvenir*, 11th November

Germany: *Volkstrauertag*, 3rd Sunday in November

 **Great Britain:** Armistice Day, 11th November; Remembrance Day, closest Sunday to 11th November

Italy: *Giorno della Vittoria*, 4th November

 Netherlands: *Wapenstilstand*, 11th November

New Zealand: ANZAC Day, 25th April; Remembrance Day, 11th November

 **United States:** Memorial Day, last Monday in May; Veterans' Day, 11th November

Timeline

1882   Germany, Austria and Italy form an alliance.

1907   Britain, France and Russia form an alliance.

1914   **28th June** Archduke Franz Ferdinand of Austria is shot dead in Sarajevo, Serbia.
28th July Austria declares war on Serbia.
August Europe goes to war.
Russia invades Germany.
Germany advances into Belgium.
September Allies stop the German advance at the first Battle of the Marne.
October Trench warfare starts on the Western Front.
The first Battle of Ypres begins.
November The Allies blockade Germany with ships.
25th December Truce declared by soldiers on the Western Front.

1915   **January** Germany sends Zeppelins to bomb Britain.
February German U-boats begin attacking Allied ships.
April Campaign at Gallipoli starts.

Second battle of Ypres starts.
May German U-boat sinks the
Lusitania passenger ship.

1916 **January** Britain begins conscription:
young men are made to enlist.
July–November The Battle of the
Somme. Britain's first use of tanks.

1917 **April** America declares war on
Germany after their ships are sunk.
Mutinies in the French army.
July–November Third Battle of
Ypres; Battle of Passchendaele.
September British mutiny at Etaples.
November Russia makes peace.
December Rationing in Britain. The
"turnip winter" in Germany.

1918 **March** Masssive German attack on
Western Front. Allies driven back.
July–August Allies fight back.
October German troops mutiny.
3rd November Austria-Hungary
signs peace agreement with Allies.
11th November Germany signs
peace agreement with Allies.

1919 **18th January** Peace talks in Paris.
11th November The first two
minutes' silence in Britain to
remember the war dead.

Glossary

blockade Something that stops people or goods reaching a place.

conscientious objector Someone who refuses to fight in a war because they do not agree with it.

enlist To join the army, navy or air force.

Front The place where armies face and fight one another.

neutral If you are neutral, you do not support either side in a war.

patriotic If you are patriotic, you are proud of your country.

rationing When the government limits the amount of food each person can buy.

trench foot A disease of the foot that comes from standing in cold water for a very long time.

trench fever A fever that causes pain in your muscles.

U-boat A German submarine.

Zeppelin A large German airship used for spying and bombing during the Great War.